364419

Our Global Community

**This book is to be returned on or before
the last date stamped below.**

PROJECTS

D1347676

Education Service

780
EAS

Falkirk Council

LIBRARY

www.heinemann.co.uk/library

Visit our website to find out more information about Heinemann Library books.

To order:

☎ Phone 44 (0) 1865 888066

📄 Send a fax to 44 (0) 1865 314091

🖥 Visit the Heinemann Bookshop at www.heinemann.co.uk/library to browse our catalogue and order online.

First published in Great Britain by Heinemann Library, Halley Court, Jordan Hill, Oxford OX2 8EJ, part of Harcourt Education. Heinemann is a registered trademark of Harcourt Education Ltd.

© Harcourt Education Ltd 2007
First published in paperback in 2008
The moral right of the proprietor has been asserted.

All rights reserved. No part of this publication may be reproduced, stored in a retrieval system, or transmitted in any form or by any means, electronic, mechanical, photocopying, recording, or otherwise, without either the prior written permission of the publishers or a licence permitting restricted copying in the United Kingdom issued by the Copyright Licensing Agency Ltd, 90 Tottenham Court Road, London W1T 4LP (www.cla.co.uk).

Editorial: Diyan Leake
Design: Joanna Hinton-Malivoire
Picture research: Ruth Smith
Production: Duncan Gilbert

Origination: Chroma Graphics (Overseas) Pte Ltd
Printed and bound in China by South China Printing Company Ltd

ISBN 978 0 431 19109 6 (hardback)
11 10 09 08 07
10 9 8 7 6 5 4 3 2 1

ISBN 978 0 431 19118 8 (paperback)
12 11 10 09
10 9 8 7 6 5 4 3 2

British Library Cataloguing in Publication Data
Easterling, Lisa
    Music. - (Our global community)
    1. Music - Juvenile literature
    780.9

Acknowledgements

The publishers would like to thank the following for permission to reproduce photographs: Alamy pp. **15** (Mauricio-José Schwarz), **16** (AAD Worldwide Travel Images); Corbis pp. **4** (Tim Pannell), **6** (Gideon Mendel), **7** (Jim Zuckerman), **9** (Richard T. Nowitz), **10** (M.A.Pushpa Kumara/epa), **11** (Gavriel Jecan), **14** (Free Agents Limited), **17** (Royalty Free), **19** (Bruce Connolly), **20** (Bob Sacha), **21** (Lindsay Hebberd); Eyewire pp. **21** (musical instrument images); Getty Images pp. **5** (National Geographic), **8** (Stone), **12** (Robert Harding World Imagery), **13** (Blend Images), **18** (Photonica).

Cover photograph of boys playing flutes in the Andes Mountains, Peru reproduced with permission of Getty Images/Imagebank.

Every effort has been made to contact copyright holders of any material reproduced in this book. Any omissions will be rectified in subsequent printings if notice is given to the publishers.

Contents

FALKIRK COUNCIL
LIBRARY SUPPORT
FOR SCHOOLS

Music around the world

All around the world, people make music.

People make music in different ways.

People make music by clapping their hands.

People make music by stomping
their feet.

People make music by singing.

People make music by playing
musical instruments.

How people play instruments

People play musical instruments with their hands.

People play drums with their hands.

People play musical instruments
with their fingers.

People play the guitar with
their fingers.

People play the bagpipes with their mouth and fingers.

People play the flute with their mouth and fingers.

People play music together.

People play music alone.

Why people play music

People play music to celebrate.

People play music on special days.

People play music to dance to.

People play music for fun.

Musical instruments

Instruments
with strings

Instruments that
you blow

Instruments that
you hit or shake

Picture glossary

 **celebrate** show that you are happy about something

 **instrument** something that you play to make music

FALKIRK COUNCIL
LIBRARY SUPPORT
FOR SCHOOLS

Index

Notes for parents and teachers
Before reading
Talk to the children about the kind of music they like to listen to. Does anyone in the family play a musical instrument?
After reading
Singing the sound. Sing the song: "Oh we can play on the big bass drum and this is the way we do it / Boom! Boom! Boom! goes the big bass drum and that's the way we do it." Encourage the children to choose an instrument and make the sound, such as "plink, plink, plonk" for a piano and so on.
The sound of instruments. Listen to a recording of "Peter and the Wolf'' by Prokofiev. Talk about how the instruments represent the different characters.
What's the instrument? Provide a range of percussion instruments, such as drums, tambourine, and guiro. Ask one child to hide from view and strike one of the instruments. Can the others guess which instrument it is?